Empty Those
POCKETS

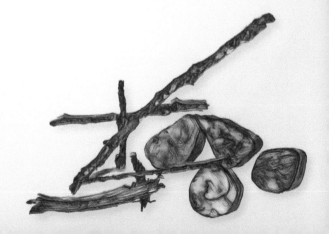

Empty Those POCKETS

Things I Learned About My Sons In the Laundry Room

Written and Illustrated by
JoAnn Coburn

Empty Those Pockets: Things I learned about my sons in the laundry room.

Published by Publish Authority
300 Colonial Center Parkway, Suite 100
Roswell, GA 30076
www.PublishAuthority.com

JoAnn Coburn, Author
EMPTY THOSE POCKETS
JOANN COBURN

ISBN: 978-1-954000-42-1 (hardcover)
ISBN: 978-1-954000-44-5 (paperback)
ISBN: 978-1-954000-43-8 (ebook)

BIO026000   (BIOGRAPHY & AUTOBIOGRAPHY / Personal Memoirs)
FAM032000   (FAMILY & RELATIONSHIPS / Parenting / Motherhood)

Book Design by Michelle M. White

Publish Authority

Dedicated to my sons
Harrison Coburn
and Carson Coburn

My two little boys
sent from Heaven above.

Taking care of your needs
was a labor of love.

With a special thank you to Jill Polisner.

Some carrots, raisins and kibbles from Spot.
So much to keep hold of for such a young tot.

A day at the park for a curious toddler
means treasures galore for a venturesome dawdler.

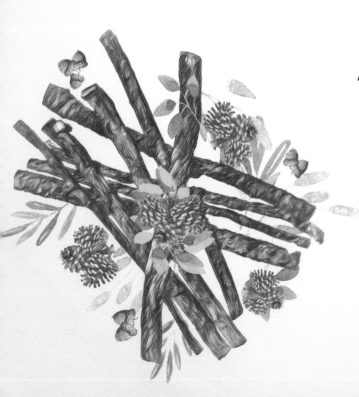

After gathering sticks,
pebbles and stones,
he discovers pockets were
not made for pinecones.

FISHING LINE

The journey through boyhood stocked
with memories to make.
Such as going fishing
with Dad at the lake.

Before casting those jeans into the machine,
I'm glad I took that little peek.
As bits and bobs were reeled from those pockets
whence havoc would surely have wreaked.

4

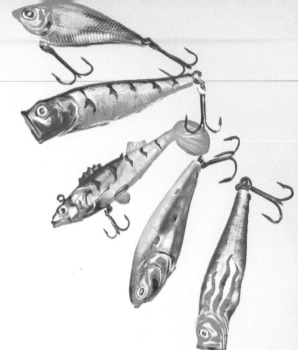

Lures, floats, worms and a sinker

were kept close at hand by this little stinker.

Make the catch of the day by taking that look.

Troll through those pockets and stay off the hook!

Hauled from those pants while searching for stains,

race cars in every pocket, one for each lane.

Ignited with colors so bright and so glorious.

Emblazoned to be iconic, legendary and notorious.

A tidal race with the washer
  could be the final lap.
Hopes of victory down the drain,
    in tiny pieces of scrap.

Make that pit stop
    to examine and inspect,
  to keep those hot rods
      from becoming a wreck.

Galactic troopers and super-heroes, action on the go!
Quests created in a flash, when figures are in tow.

Charged by thought, a battle is fought,
and the villains are kept at bay.
But an ill-fated wrangle in the laundry room
may zap their powers away.

If tossed inside to tumble on high,
    along with your attire.
Doomed they'd be, as you will see,
    even superhumans melt in the dryer.

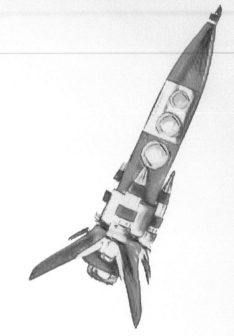

Be a hero and save the day
by emptying out those pockets.

Don't forget the capes, masks,
spaceships and the rockets.

Sports cards and tickets,
some signed by a player.
An ageless show and tell of sorts
unless hosed by a hard-hitting sprayer.

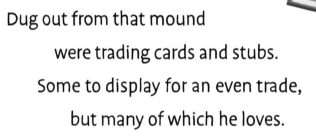

Dug out from that mound
were trading cards and stubs.
Some to display for an even trade,
but many of which he loves.

Play it safe and don't take a chance
because an all-star line-up
could be in the seat of those pants.

Tackle those pockets and you might retrieve
an autograph from a rookie or an MVP.

Slam dunked and dribbled upon.
Whitewashed in one big swoop.
Thrown out of bounds, causing a big upset
by a shot into the washer hoop.

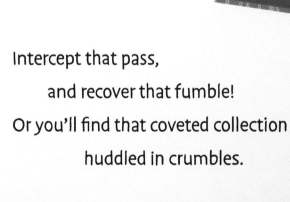

Intercept that pass,
and recover that fumble!
Or you'll find that coveted collection
huddled in crumbles.

Your boy has grown into a "tween,"
and the pursuit never ceases
    to keep those clothes clean.

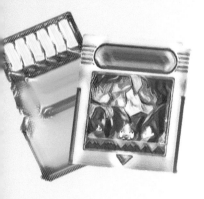

Devices, games and even a phone.
A costly mistake if in the washer they're thrown.

The heavier the pants,
the chances are higher
that the stuff in those pockets
doesn't belong in the dryer.

Checking, you'll see, could save you
some cash
for electronic repairs from that
unfortunate splash!

Throughout those teen years
thoughts entered my mind.
I might not be happy
with the contents I'd find.

Proudly, I can say there was no need for such fears.

Because good values outweighed

the pressure of peers.

A developing body and a changing mindset.
Those years when the laundry smelled
like a pile of sweat!

Urged to dash in and toss those clothes
as fast as you can, while holding your nose.

Take my advice and avoid the
temptation,
because things in those pockets
can cause a sticky situation.

Suddenly a change of pocket contents.
Bubble gum is replaced by a container of mints.

Essentials for grooming to keep the girls swooning,
are kept at his fingertips.
Stuff for his hair is always right there,
just in case he needs a quick fix.

Comb through those pockets for lip balm and gel.
A hot mess, indeed, if in the dryer they fell.

Self image set in motion, upon starting high school.
When silly and cute suddenly evolves
into stylish and cool.

Deep in his pockets were notes to his crush.
Filled with tender sentiment and
young love mush.

Scribed to the girl who captured his heart
and made him feel so smitten.
But head over heels into troubled water
may erase those sweet words written.

To spare him the embarrassment
of my unintended view
I saved that load for him to do.

Empty those pockets of things worth saving.
This scoop of advice will keep memories
from fading.

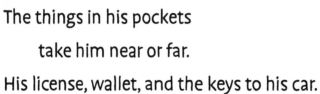

The things in his pockets
     take him near or far.
His license, wallet, and the keys to his car.

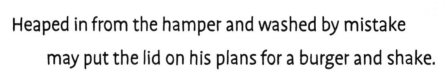

Heaped in from the hamper and washed by mistake
     may put the lid on his plans for a burger and shake.

Torn up and twisted, left by accident
his bank cards will re-surface all warped and bent.

Receipts and a paycheck all soaked to pieces.

To be plucked from socks, shirts and fleeces.

There's much on the line if you fail to pre-sort

as you may never know where he'd stashed his passport!

A visit from college may not end his laundry.

A bittersweet task you've endured with a quandary.

Had a hunch after seeing those bags of washables,

he could still use some help as he becomes more responsible.

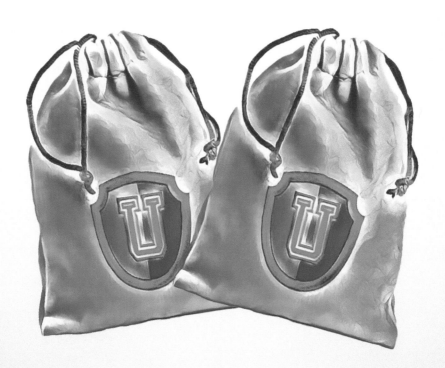

A step has been taken to independence you see,
but you still find his dorm card and student ID.

In a perfect world, he should check on his own.
But cut him some slack and enjoy
    having him home!

Delight in knowing he still needs you sometimes,
as the foothold of the ladder to manhood, he climbs.

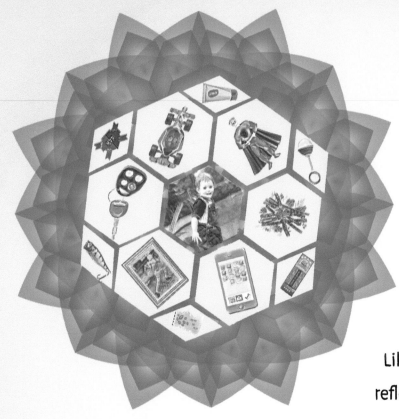

The signal has sounded
    that my spin cycle has spun.
I've thrown in the towel
    and my dirty work is done!

Like an ever-changing kaleidoscope
reflects light as it's turned,
new patterns appeared
as my sons grew and matured.

Through a mother's lens of love, I saw a spectacular design.
Soaking in the splendor of each fragment of time.

Things I learned in the laundry room
were not the details you might have assumed.

Among those treasures I was lucky to find
joy, peace and gratitude
hidden deep down inside.

So, call a time out
from the daily grind
to pause, reflect
and recenter your mind.

Unveilings of childhood
as I watched it unfold
became the formula I needed
to balance my load.

Another season follows as we anticipate
the birth of a child to celebrate.

This aspiring grandma will be bursting with joy
at a baby shower for a girl or a boy.

Friends and family
all playing silly games,
chatting of nursery colors
and baby names.

Advice and tips
   being launched like rockets.

To my son I whispered,
   Empty those Pockets!

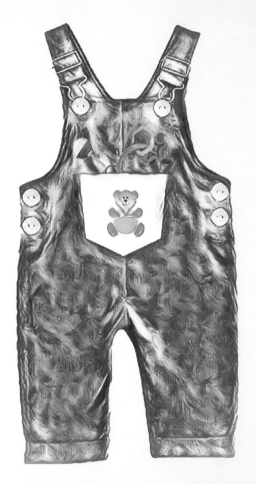

About the Author

JoAnn Coburn is a native of Atlanta, Georgia, where she and her husband have raised their two sons, Harrison and Carson. She struck the perfect balance between career and family as a freelance graphic artist. *Empty Those Pockets: Things I Learned About My Sons in the Laundry Room* embodies and weaves these two important aspects of her life together through her illustrations and tales of her sons' childhoods.

JoAnn has a fond appreciation of art and music, and she enjoys crafting, travelling, and entertaining in her home.